THE SOCIOLOGY
OF THE ABSURD

OR:

The Application
of Professor X

*Annotated with an Introduction
and Postscript*
by

DANIEL J. BOORSTIN

724614

SIMON AND SCHUSTER
New York

FIRST PRINTING

SBN 671-20499-8
Library of Congress Catalog Card Number: 70-107247
Designed by Irving Perkins
Manufactured in the United States of America
Printed by Mahony & Roese, Inc., New York, N.Y.
Bound by American Book-Stratford Press, New York, N.Y.

Contents

THE APPLICATION OF PROFESSOR X
(In full and unabridged form, precisely as it was rejected by the Institute for Democratic Studies)

APPENDICES

8   CONTENTS

Never interfere with the enemy when he is in the process of destroying himself.

—Napoleon

INTRODUCTION
by
DANIEL J. BOORSTIN

———————◆———————

I well remember the chilly
Monday morning in November when my weekly manila
envelope marked "Confidential" from the Institute for
Democratic Studies brought, among other items, the document that everybody is now privileged to read in this
slim volume. For some years I have served on the selecting
committee of the Institute to help pick projects worthy of
support by the income from the ten million dollars recently left by the Wallerstein Foundation "to alleviate
human misery, promote democracy, and intensify human
dignity." It is giving away no secrets to say that the
mine-run of applications for our support has been pretty
prosaic. They have generally lacked originality. They
have lacked social significance and intellectual promise. It
goes without saying, however, that a sufficient number of
them have given definite promise of spending (in a fashion
acceptable to our accountants and to the Internal Revenue
Service) the substantial sums which we are required to
dispose of.

Imagine my delight and relief, then, after three years'
service for the Institute, at finding at least one application
that had some thrust, some imagination, some élan. This

project, moreover, actually seemed focused on the major problems of American democracy today! The application, which follows, was submitted anonymously. It was signed "Professor X," with nothing but a postoffice box as the address to which the Institute should write if the project proved acceptable. At that time, the covering letter explained, the authors of the proposal would be willing to reveal their identities.

Needless to say, that time never came. For I was alone in urging that we support the Professor X project. All that the authors were requesting was the sum of $3,420 for a Feasibility Study to be undertaken under their supervision and with the cooperation of the several *ad hoc* student-faculty committees mentioned in the application.

I could not persuade my colleagues on the Institute's selecting committee. Their first objection, of course, was to the anonymity of the application. ("We give our grants to people, not to ideas," one of them remarked.) They naturally objected, too, to the smallness of the sum involved. The Institute's Executive Director, who is always present at our meetings, pointed out that (counting overhead, travel expenses of committee members, long-distance phone calls, postage, etc.) it costs a minimum of $4,500 to process *any* application for Institute support. How wasteful, he insisted, to expend this amount for a project that might result in the out-of-pocket expenditure by the Foundation of only $3,420. He said it seemed to him this would be a case of "penny-wise and pound-foolish."

Finally (I suspect this was conclusive), my colleagues objected that even if the project had not had these two strikes against it, the essential idea was foolish. Why? Their answer was that the applicants were really not asking us to support a research project at all, but simply a *reductio ad absurdum*. Those "callow" scholars who had drawn up the application, my colleagues insisted, had forfeited, by the very nature of their proposal, any right to respect or support by the learned community. The applicants were proposing to take the most respectable and most unexceptionable tenets of right-thinking liberalism and contemporary social science, and make them look ridiculous by pushing them to an absurd extreme.

So the application was refused out of hand. Our Executive Director did not even show the courtesy of sending to Professor X's postoffice box address the usual cordially regretful rejection.

I disagreed, on all counts. I simply could not follow the "economy" argument. I found the essential ideas in the application extremely interesting, and even courageous. The applicants were proposing to press to their logical conclusions some widely current—in fact almost universally accepted—ideas. In an age when the Theater of the Absurd has taught us so much, I asked, why should we refuse to be instructed by the Sociology of the Absurd?

Therefore I thought it our duty to give the applicants the small grant they had requested. Under the circumstances, I urged, the anonymity of the applicants was not only understandable. It was actually fortunate. Here, for once, we would have the opportunity to judge the essential merits of a project apart from personalities. But I got nowhere with my colleagues, and I assumed the project was dead.

Then, to my astonishment, I read in the October 1969 *Esquire* a bowdlerized and mercilessly abridged version of that application by Professor X. The editors of *Esquire*, as they explained in their note (reprinted below) to their version of the application, had secured the text through devious channels.

My first reaction was to be amazed and disappointed that the uncompromising Professor X (whom I had not and still have not met, but whose case I had argued at such length) should have agreed to the publication of any but the fullest, most accurate version of his proposal. Then, on second thought, it appeared perfectly consistent with the circumstances described by *Esquire* that Professor X had never been consulted by them, nor even given his consent to the publication in that form.

After some hard thinking about all the moral implications involved, and after consulting with my wife and a few close friends, I decided it was my duty to secure publication of the full text. I suggested to my friend Richard Kluger at Simon and Schuster that he could perform a public service by publishing a full and unabridged version of this interesting document.

Publication, I explained, would have a double edge. Not only would it give a wide audience to the important suggestions of Professor X. It would also, incidentally (at a time when the tax status of foundations is under scrutiny), reveal the kind of bookkeeping that some foundations use, and the kind of pusillanimity that foundations sometimes show in choosing the projects for their support. Though preoccupied with other matters, when Richard Kluger quickly embraced my suggestion, I volunteered to turn from those other tasks and help in any way I could.

The reader will find, then, that pursuant to the suggestions of Simon and Schuster I have edited Professor X's
application and have tried to place it in the larger context
of American intellectual history.

This action on my part is in no way intended as a criticism, direct or implied, of those particular colleagues who
have served with me on the selecting committee. Nor is
it my special purpose to single out the Institute for adverse
criticism. I would hope, too, that they would not consider
this publication a breach of the confidentiality of the applications and supporting material which our committee
continues to receive. Should my colleagues disagree, I
would cheerfully (as I here do publicly) offer my resig-
nation from the committee. But I feel that my duty as a
citizen overrides all others, and that has required me to
join in this publication.

The editors at Simon and Schuster and I have been im-
pressed by the urgency of the subjects treated, and by
the speed with which events are moving in the United
States today. Therefore we have felt that, if this document was to be published at all, it should be published
immediately. It has been possible to move so quickly only
because my wife, Ruth F. Boorstin, has helped even more
than usual. In the brief time allotted I have added to the
text some minor embellishments, such as the motto and
the dedication. Wherever a statement is by me, I have so
indicated. All the rest of the text, including the Ap-
pendices, is by Professor X, and was found in the original application. The pressure of time has meant, inevitably,
that it has not been possible for me to provide as full

annotation as I might have liked. Nor, indeed, have I been allowed leisure to give that final double-check to all the references which every scholar considers his duty. We hope that readers will charitably bear this in mind while they keep in the foreground the vast and crucial issues raised in this remarkable document.

THE *ESQUIRE* EDITORS' NOTE

Some few months ago at one of the largest universities in the Middle West, the local SDS chapter and a group of sympathetic students occupied the Social Sciences building for forty-eight hours. While there, they indulged in the usual rifling of files in search of evidence linking the faculty with the Defense Department, the CIA, etc. The following memorandum was found in the desk of one of the university's leading sociology professors. To its dismay, the SDS discovered that this professor and a number of his colleagues were on their side. *Accordingly the memorandum was suppressed by the militant students and has only become available for publication here through channels which cannot be disclosed. Also, lest the sociologist lose his tenure, the editors have chosen not to reveal his name.*

THE APPLICATION
OF PROFESSOR X

*(In full and unabridged form,
precisely as it was rejected by
the Institute for Democratic Studies)*

Prologue to New Democracy

—————◆—————

THESE proposals would never have come about if we had not been a thoroughly *un*representative group of the faculty. They are the product of many meetings of a small self-appointed group in the social sciences. We began our conferences only a few years ago with the first glimmerings of New Democracy in the rise of Students for a Democratic Society on our campus. We—a small cadre of dedicated, concerned social scientists—have decided to take a leaf out of the book of our brightest students. They have wisely preferred immediate action toward New Democracy, in place of letting themselves be "sicklied o'er with the pale cast of thought." We have determined (despite our imprisonment within a repressive institution) not to allow ourselves to be intimidated by our older, reactionary colleagues.

For some months, therefore, we have been meeting secretly at one or another of our homes. Our constant single aim has been a plan of *action*. Any ideas appearing here are a mere by-product of that single-minded search. While it may seem only a short step from the New Left to the New Democracy, it is indeed a long leap. We have tried to take that leap—not by being more ideological or more thought-sicklied than our young leaders, but by envisioning the great promise that the social sciences can offer to all oppressed peoples. We like to think that what we were engaged in—and in a sense perhaps have quite accidentally invented—is the "Think-In."

The next decade will witness the most remarkable redefinition of Americanism in all our history. We refer, of course, to "New Democracy." Its origins are many and varied. Some may find them in the Supreme Court decisions beginning about 1954; others may trace them to the Martin Luther King riots of April 1968; still others to the promising emergence of our new Homeopathic Social Science. And relevant, too, is the rumored perfection of an inexpensive, pocketable, silent telescope-sighted rifle. But our purpose is not to find origins—rather, to find the stream of development so that we (along with all students, social scientists, and citizens) can better swim with it.

Each of the five parts in this brief report proposes another element of New Democracy. Trained as social scientists, we have naturally started with the most specific and most concrete and moved on to the broader and the more general. In ours, as in any other effective wide-spectrum program, there may at first appear to be certain inconsistencies. As in any other revolutionary new conceptual framework, there has been a need to give old terms a new meaning and to invent new terms to emphasize our new meaning. We ask only that our readers bear with us and hear us out to the end, with a patience proportionate to the magnitude of the subject and the greatness of the issues. They will then, hopefully, see how our several discrete suggestions are knit together toward the largest and most universal objectives. If our social-scientist colleagues, accustomed to pedantic nit-picking, can be persuaded to reserve *their* judgment, they too may find fruitful new ways in which they may use a New Social Science to promote New Democracy.

· I ·
Ethnic Proportionalism:
The "E.Q." and Its Uses

WE are, as the cliché goes, "a nation of immigrants." But the Establishment-endorsed ideals of assimilation and integration have long misled us into trying to forget who we *really* are.

New Democracy will help us discover that "We are not what we are but where we came from." Or, in other words: "There can be no more shallow or short-sighted view than that which seeks the guidelines for our national future in the present, in the immediate past, or in the future itself. The guidelines to the fulfillment of each American lie deep in his own ethnic past. The deeper we dig—the farther back we reach—the more reliable and more fruitful for each of us." (E. R. Brown, *The Black Ethic and Multiple Ethnicity*, New York, 1968, page 76.)

Christianity itself teaches us that the most important facts are the *earliest*. In the Beginning, God created man, and then man lived briefly in the Garden of

Eden, and then he sinned.* Are not these the most important and most universal facts, which dwarf all the
puny later events? The corollary is that each and every
one of us can fulfill himself only by being ever more
constantly and more vividly aware of where he came
from—in the beginning. By this we do not, of course,
mean him personally, but his remote ancestors. As our
social scientists have shown, the more remote the time
and place the more deeply and permanently have their
influence become ingrained in the "soul" (in the new
ethnic sense). And the more essential it is then that
each person's ethnic origins be marked off and measured by the best available quantitative techniques.

How can we apply these truths to American life? It
is not easy. Some have simple-mindedly supposed that
the problem could be solved by the mere expedient
of ethnic (or racial) separatism. In the 1960's the pioneer work of the Black Muslims, the Black Panthers,
the Black Students Union, and other sympathetic
groups (SNCC, CORE, etc.) has carried forward the
spirit of the earlier Ku Klux Klan pioneers and has
helped set our modern direction. Their approach has
been admirable, but, like many pioneers, they have

---

* A succinct illustration of the vivid awareness of the merging of past and present accentuated by the imperial conflicts
of the last century is Sir Charles Napier's famous dispatch to
the British Colonial Office after his capture (1843) of the In-
dian provincial capital of Hyderabad in Sind: "*Peccavi*"
(from the Latin *pecco, peccare*, to sin). Napier himself translated this "I have Sind." ED.

oversimplified the problems. They have taken a "black and white" approach. Their answer is "either/or." The program of black schools for blacks, white schools for whites, etc., has been a glorious experiment, and a first step toward ethnic self-fulfillment. It surely can save countless black souls from the indignity of being taught by whites, and can save them the time-wasting, soul-soiling experience of reading books written by whites or hearing any ideas except those that are pure black—and vice versa.

But the goal of ethnic self-fulfillment for our *whole* society is much more complicated. That is why we advocate (and have begun to develop the details of) a more ethnically universal program. In this we are guided by the New Democratic motto, "Every Soul Its Own Role."

At first sight the most logical solution would seem to be a separate school for each ethnic group. Yet easy solutions produce difficult problems. Perhaps it will not be too hard to find enough Italian teachers to man the Italian schools, enough Jewish teachers for the Jewish schools, enough German teachers for the German schools. But we may face a near-insoluble problem in finding enough Belgian teachers for young Belgo-Americans or enough Korean teachers for young Korean-Americans, etc.

Another problem will arise from the complex backgrounds of the students themselves. Imagine a youngster with an Irish-American mother and an Italian-

American father. And imagine, too, that his mother and his father each have one Polish-American grandparent. In this situation the child's ethnic makeup is $\frac{2}{8}$ (or $\frac{1}{4}$) Polish, $\frac{3}{8}$ Irish, and $\frac{3}{8}$ Italian. It would be a violation of the integral personality of a child to require him to attend a school whose ethnic makeup was not the same as his own. Accordingly, every parent should have the option of sending his child to whatever school in his opinion has an ethnic makeup best suited to the ethnic makeup of the child. It should be the duty of the local school board to provide transportation of the child to any such selected school within the state of the child's residence or within any contiguous state, but not farther. Yet we all know how much litigation and public agitation and expense this can give rise to.

Therefore, our group gives high priority to the development of new techniques that will more perfectly and more economically fulfill the ethnic idealism of New Democracy. Here we have a quite concrete proposal, based on some of the more spectacular recent breakthroughs of social science (especially in the application of quantitative methodology), which the present oppressive structure of our universities has prevented from receiving the publicity it deserves. The new principle is thoroughly programmatic in nature. We call it "Ethnic Proportionalism."

Ethnic Proportionalism is in essence an extremely simple idea. Its basic new tool, which we now offer with no little diffidence, will be the "Ethnic Quotient" (or E.Q.) for each individual. The E.Q. has obvious similarities to the I.Q. (Intelligence Quotient), which we know so well and which, at least until recently, has performed such yeoman service among the social sciences. But the E.Q. is a much subtler concept, and hence provides a much subtler tool. For while, as many social scientists have come to believe, the I.Q. is *merely* quantitative and self-confirming ("Intelligence tests test what intelligence tests test"), the E.Q. is qualitative and soul-fulfilling.

Drawing on genealogy, skin-pigmentation tests, somatometric and physiognometric devices, and linguistic and attitudinal measurements, and other data, the E.Q. provides a keyed series of numbers accurately indicative of each individual's ethnicity. Each individual's E.Q. can then be conveniently noted on his or her Social Security card and can thus become the permanent basis for his proper institutional treatment—in ways not violating his true ethnicity. Since a person's E.Q. (like his I.Q.) never changes, the data, once registered at birth, need never be revised. Of course, it is essential to the very idea of ethnicity that no accidental fact (such as a person removing to another country or changing his religion or speaking another language) can have the slightest effect. The E.Q., moreover, has the same advantages over the I.Q. that the Library of Congress book-classification system has over the Dewey Decimal system: it is more concise and the quotient itself furnishes an immediate clue to the whole character of the classified individual.

For example, take the young man whom we will call Patrick Fiorello Ginsburg. His E.Q. is J64:Med 23:G13. Translated into common parlance we may say that young Ginsburg is 64 per cent Jewish, 23 per cent Italian ("Med" = Mediterranean), and 13 per cent Irish ("G" = Gaelic). A special practical advantage of the E.Q., illustrated in this case, is that closely related ethnic groups are pulled together so that the appropriate special treatment can be given *all* of them even if some components of the group are not numerous enough to warrant special treatment for each of them alone. Thus, for example, "Med" (for Mediterranean) includes Italians, Corsicans, Syrians, Tunisians, and White Abyssinians, and "G" (for Gaelic) includes Irish and Scots.

Note that the E.Q. is concerned not with absolutes but only with *relative* ethnicity, that is to say with the *proportions* of different ethnic elements in the individual. Therefore the E.Q. is always stated with the largest element first and other items in descending order. The numerals in any person's E.Q. always add up to 100.

Our little group, with its extremely limited resources, has hardly scratched the surface in finding applications for this remarkable new tool. We will suggest a few possible rational uses, mainly in the area of education, because that is where we have had the most experience. But we are confident that others, equally well qualified in their areas, will find myriad new applications of no less significance.

(a) *Schoolteachers and classroom instruction.* In the case of young Ginsburg, for example, new refinements could be introduced into the classroom fulfillment of his ethnicity. In place of his spending *all* his time in a Jewish school (as he would under the proposed new School Disintegration Program) and so neglecting the other, minor elements of his ethnicity, now his classroom time would be clearly and precisely divided (as calculated by computers into which the ethnically annotated Social Security cards could be fed). He will spend a proportion of his time exactly equal to the requirements of his E.Q. under the classroom instruction of a "J," a "Med," or a "G" teacher. (Temporarily—or at least until a large enough pool of ethnically diversified teachers could be accumulated— a useful expedient, already tried with impressive success for other purposes, would be team-teaching.)

(b) *School lunches and ethnic cuisine.* Instead of each schoolchild eating *all* his school lunches in the cuisine of his predominant ethnic makeup (as, nowadays, well-brought-up black youngsters are encouraged to eat lunches of coconut, bananas, and other African cuisine, Italian youngsters to eat lunches of spaghetti, ravioli, with an occasional pizza for those of southern Italian origin, etc.), the child of the future could have the benefit of much more variety, which would still fulfill his true ethnicity. Young Ginsburg, for example, could have nearly one-quarter of his meals of "Med" cuisine, which might include a farinaceous Italian dish with an occasional couscous, and for still more variety he would have about an eighth of his meals in wholesome Irish style. Incidentally, of course, this would tend to alleviate the relatively high content of polyunsaturated fats found in salami, blintzes, and the other elements of "J" cuisine. But the physiological benefits would be relatively unimportant compared to the psychological benefits. If the guidelines of his E.Q. were followed, no child would be deprived of the opportunity to nourish himself on "soul" food in the fullest ethnic sense of the word. Every child would have what we might call an ethnically balanced diet.

(c) *Holidays.*   The fixing and celebration of holidays has posed some of the most difficult and increasingly complex administrative problems of our schools. These problems are apt to become even more complex with the further development of the School Disintegration Program. They touch the whole economy, but most obviously affect the calculations of officials charged with public transportation, with public parks and playgrounds, etc., not to mention the problems of fixing contractual terms with teachers' unions when the number of holidays in a given school during a given academic year is so unpredictable. In the future, the reliable E.Q. figures for the whole school population would enable the authorities to calculate in advance how many children would be expected to be absent on Chaim Weizmann's birthday, how many on Mussolini's birthday, how many on Malcolm X's birthday, how many on Franco's birthday, and there would even be a small enough margin of error to estimate that small number who might still absent themselves on Washington's or Lincoln's birthday.

(d) *Language arts and foreign languages.* As our educationists have finally come to recognize, it is hard to find a good reason for teaching foreign languages. With the possible exception of Chinese, all past written languages have been media of past Establishments. And in the past even all spoken languages, because of Establishment-enforced taboos against "obscenities," and against the description of sexual acts and acts of physical elimination, have somehow lacked vitality. Nevertheless a proper ethnic orientation can give purpose to the teaching of foreign languages (if only they are no longer considered "foreign" languages) that will justify their inclusion in the curriculum. One reason why youngsters have not been motivated to learn languages other than that miscalled "their own" is simply that the proper ethnic content of language arts has been disparaged or ignored. By the use of the E.Q. a youngster's time could be proportioned among the various languages relevant to his ethnicity. Of course, the emphasis must always be on the relevant *folk* languages, *folk* literature, and *folk* song. It goes without saying, then, that Plattdeutsch (*Low* German) must be preferred to Hochdeutsch (*High* German), Old French (of Villon and the troubadours) must be preferred to the Latinate pseudo-French of the Académie, Old Icelandic (of the Eddas) must be preferred to modern literary Danish, Swedish, or Norwegian, Swahili must be preferred to Coptic or to Hausa, etc., etc. A youngster of mixed ethnicity (and hence of mixed motivation) could be expected, say, to learn only two cantos of the *Nibelungenlied*, devoting the rest of his language arts time to a few score verses of *The Song of Roland*, with perhaps a book or two of the folk-Croatian version of the *Odyssey*. From this point of view, shorter items (e.g. "O Tannenbaum!," "La Marseillaise," Old English Ballads like "Sir Hugh," etc.) are best suited to arrangement for the mixed ethnic soul-needs of any especially mixed-up students.

Perhaps the greatest national service of the E.Q. would be to provide an ethnically scientific alternative to the complex problems of total ethnic separatism. The growing movement to distribute all the states of the Union proportionately among the major ethnic groups poses all sorts of difficulties. Not the least of these is its failure to take sufficient account of the large number of ethnic hybrids. It would be a gross injustice to the vast number of Americans (our census data are not sufficiently precise to permit an exact estimate) who are ethnically mixed through no fault of their own, to condemn them to become "second-class citizens." And that, of course, is what would happen after they were arbitrarily assigned to that particular new ethnic state to which their predominant makeup would allocate them. The E.Q. now makes possible the fullest ethnic fulfillment of each individual *in proportion to* his or her essential ethnic makeup—and still substantially within the framework of the Federal Union. This is the true promise of Ethnic Proportionalism.

· II ·
Toward a More Refined
System of Intergenerational
Bookkeeping

NEW Democracy requires not only that we reform and refine our concept of ethnicity (discovering, meanwhile, its implications for our system of education and all our other institutions), but that we update our concept of justice. Here, again, some of the unheralded breakthroughs in recent social science offer us a grand new opportunity. Our little cadre now suggests only the merest prolegomena to an outline of these new possibilities.

This seems to be the age in which we have finally discovered the means to express quantitatively even the subtlest* qualitative facts. We would do less than

---

* Without directly contradicting this generalization by Professor X, it may be worth asking whether even some of the wisest men of our age may have lost sight of Aristotle's prudent counsel that wisdom in discussing *any* subject requires that we speak with no more precision than the subject admits of. The prevailing spirit of our time, which Professor X here describes, and in the course of his Application amply

justice to our few imaginative colleagues among social scientists if we did not here acknowledge our great debt for much of what follows in this section to the scandalously unpublicized researches of a brilliant little group in the Department of Ethics of this university.

The key concept here is the idea of the "Merit Quotient" (M.Q.). The Merit Quotient is in essence nothing more nor less than the product of a refined system of intergenerational bookkeeping. The guiding slogan is one that has begun to become familiar in the literature of the SDS, the Black Students Union, and other concerned groups: "Social Justice Through Intergenerational Justification." The *main* function of our institutions, if they are *ever* to be worthy of the epithet "democratic," must be "to Redress the Historical Imbalance." It will become apparent later in this memorandum that this is the true meaning of the New Equality. All this goes back to Darwin and Spencer and Marx in the last century and to Arnold Toynbee earlier in our own. It also aims to make into a *social* (by contrast with a mere individual or familial) reality the rather skimpy and dogmatic insights into intrafamilial generational bookkeeping offered us by Freud.

---

illustrates, is expressed in an inscription (attributed to Lord Kelvin) found carved on the outside of the Social Science Research Building (completed in 1926) of my own University of Chicago. It reads: "When you cannot measure, your knowledge is meager and unsatisfactory." I prefer the colloquial version, from my state of Oklahoma: "If you can't count it, it don't count!" ED.

With these large purposes in mind, our cadre has the temerity to offer still another new conceptual tool. We realize, of course, that in doing this each one of our group is, so to speak, laying his professional reputation on the line. But the stakes are more than worth it.

We have come to see that the new conceptual tool we offer is really the final product of a long advancing struggle—in which the common people of all ages (perhaps more than the so-called "learned") have played a seminal role. In the Middle Ages people were taught that the great issue of justice lay in the *future* (or what they called "the afterlife"), when God would reward good and punish evil. Of course this helped make them more docile in the face of all sorts of social oppressions. In early modern times a step forward was taken when people focused their attention on the *present*. But social oppressions still remained multiform, reaching even into the society's very interstices.* Now, in later modern times, by applying that principle of new social science commonly called "Progress Through Regression," we take still another step in

---

* A catchy illustration of Professor X's generalization is this rhyme expressing popular reactions to the English enclosure movement in the eighteenth century:

> *The law doth punish man or woman*
> *That steals the goose from off the common,*
> *But lets the greater felon loose,*
> *That steals the common from the goose.*

ED.

sharpening and broadening our vision of social justice. For us neither the futuristic romanticism of the Middle Ages nor the crass presentism of early modern times will do. Reaching deeper into ourselves—by which, of course, we mean our ethnic past—we now seek a wider justice.

We aim at the Historical Equation: All the *past* injustices (in our "Pre-Life") must be balanced by adequate present compensations. New Democracy aims to fulfill this equation for each and every individual.

Therefore, the persons who (in their ancestors) most suffered or were most disadvantaged in the past, must be specially privileged and advantaged in the present. Contrariwise those who were *over*privileged in the past (in the persons of their ancestors) must have their historical balance rectified by being made *under*privileged in the present. "The Worse the Better; the Better the Worse!"*

The large social objective then, for the first time, becomes quite clear and quite simple. We must rearrange our institutions, our distributions of pains and pleasures (if we may use a neo-Benthamite terminology), of honor and disgrace in our time, so that all the past pluses and minuses will cancel out and the product of the Historical Equation for any individual will always equal zero.

---

* Compare Voltaire: *"Le mieux est l'ennemi du bien."* ("The best is the enemy of the good.") *Dictionnaire Philosophique* (1764), "Art dramatique." ED.

The Merit Quotient (M.Q.) that we now will describe actually gives us a device for working out the
Historical Equation for each and every American, re-
gardless of race, creed, or color. The M.Q. reduces
the whole problem to manageable (and easily repli-
cated) *quantitative* proportions. What follows is a
much oversimplified explanation of how it works.
Since we are speaking here not mainly to our social-
science colleagues but to all concerned Americans, we
have felt justified in omitting certain refinements
which we have thought through but which are not
necessary for the purposes of this application to make
the essential paradigm intelligible.

The M.Q. starts from the base figure of 100, which
represents the maximum merit points that any individual could accumulate. But this maximum is a purely
theoretical possibility which we will never encounter
in living men and women. To have an M.Q. of 100 it
would be necessary for *all* a person's ancestors to have
been the victims of genocide, and presumably even before any of them had had the pleasure of procreating
children.

But the M.Q. of zero *is* a practical possibility, since
it is quite conceivable that the sufferings experienced
by a person's ancestors should be precisely balanced
by their pleasures. Notice, too, that—at a further extreme from the purely theoretical base figure of "plus
100"—it is possible, and not at all unusual, for a person
to have a *minus* M.Q. That simply means that the per-

son's ancestors have, totally speaking, accumulated more pleasure and privilege than pain and suffering.

Since we are always casting up the M.Q. in order to arrive at the Historical Equation, it is obvious that ancestral *sufferings* must be given a *plus* significance and ancestral *pleasures* a *negative* significance. Our dominant purpose is simply to see how much merit has been acquired by the individual in this way so we can assess his fair and proper special claim now to the goods, services, and honors of our present-day society.

The M.Q., then, provides rules for translating into plus and minus mathematical symbols *all* the satisfactions, privileges, pleasures, sufferings, and punishments enjoyed or undergone by anybody's ancestors. The historian and the demographer-statistician in our group have helped us develop a way to introduce the time-factor into our calculations, so that the M.Q. does not fail to take account of the number of years during which one's ancestors suffered or enjoyed the plus or minus experience. Similarly, the psychologists among us have developed a coefficient of intensity, so that the M.Q. will weigh the varying poignancies of the past experiences. The time-factor becomes a multiplicand of the quantity assigned to the experience itself. The intensity-coefficient (a larger number indicating a greater intensity) becomes the dividend for the suffering-factor and the divisor for the pleasure-factor.

For purposes of clarity, all this can be summarized in the simple formula (where I = intensity-coefficient,

T = time-factor, S = suffering, and P = pleasure):

$$\frac{I}{TS} - \frac{TP}{I} = M.Q.$$

Suffice it to say that even our preliminary work has shown the M.Q. formula to be capable of endless refinements. Such past sufferings as the periods in which the subject's ancestors were in slavery, were indentured servants, were incarcerated in ghettos or prisons —each of these is assigned a specific quantitative value. Similarly, catastrophes—such as floods, earthquakes, famines, plagues, etc.—suffered by ancestors are given appropriate numerical symbols. On the other side, periods of affluence, in which ancestors enjoyed the luxury of, say, private servants or of pleasure travel, are assigned numbers.

We would be the first to admit that there remain some ambiguities in the system. For example, how large a number will we assign to the oppressive experiences of studentship and faculty membership in universities, and how will this figure compare with that assigned to other forms of slavery? Here is an opportunity for fruitful interdisciplinary collaboration between historians and psychologists, which doubtless could be assisted by an *ad hoc* student-faculty committee. This is a challenge worthy of all our best efforts. Still, these are only problems of detail. Our group has been so thoroughly persuaded of the feasibility and urgency of this project that we have actually begun to develop a handbook (classifying and quantifying all past experiences) which is already comprehensive enough for present purposes. We are therefore in a position to state that the M.Q., as of today, is a practical possibility.

It will, of course, be a great administrative convenience that a person's M.Q., like his Social Security number, his E.Q. and his I.Q., *never* changes.* The M.Q., no less than the E.Q., is the product of the individual's somatic genealogy. The M.Q. assesses the merit attached to an individual when he comes into this world, and obviously cannot be altered one iota by "other" personal qualities of talent, education, or character, by "achievements" or "crimes." All these later items, as we now know, are anyway nothing but the product of all those past forces. If we have once accurately quantified those past forces, it is then tautologous to make separate calculations for later accidental factors. New Democracy is concerned only with each individual's *essential* merit. That is totally and accurately indicated by his M.Q.

Since the M.Q. is calculated specially for each individual it is plainly a highly individualistic paradigm. Since it draws so richly on the past it is also of course intensely traditional.

We will begin then to see some of the confusions produced until now by our failure to distinguish

---

* For a possible qualification of this generalization, see below, Appendix III, "Is 'Retributive Merit' a Useful Concept?"

sharply enough between essential merit and what has sometimes been called "competence." Competence—commonly defined as "the proven ability to complete a task"—was formerly, and erroneously, identified with merit. But now modern social science, in our research for the Historical Equation, reveals that this was a naïve and even a dangerous confusion.

Search for ever wider applications of the M.Q., constant efforts to reduce the margins of error in its calculation—these are enterprises which should engage the full energies and imaginations of social scientists everywhere. Imagine the possibilities—in selecting students for college entrance, in awarding Civil Service jobs, in choosing officers for promotion in the Armed Services and the Diplomatic Corps, and in a thousand other areas of New Democratic America. A single handy precalculated M.Q. will save time, money, paperwork, and red tape. It will also remove the bases of the old accusations of unfair discrimination, partisan patronage, and racial and religious prejudice which characterized the mid-century so-called "merit" system.*

---

* For a brief exploration of whether the E.Q.-M.Q. dichotomy is justified in practice, and for a subtle problem of sociometrics raised by the effort to combine them, see below, Appendix I, "On the Relation Between the E.Q. and the M.Q."

· III ·
Toward a More Tonic Society and a Homeopathic Social Science

———————◆———————

WHILE both Ethnic Proportionalism and Intergenerational Bookkeeping are of fundamental importance to New Democracy, they are essentially significant because they give us two new tools of social action: the E.Q. and the M.Q. Now we come to a general principle, to be followed by other general principles in the next two sections, which, despite its highly theoretical nature, is no less pregnant actionwise.

The principle we will now explain, while totally relevant to the present problems of an oppressive society and to the future promise of New Democray, lay hidden in the entrails of history until only recently. We are proud to be the agents of its resurrection—or perhaps "renascence" would be a better word. In the mid-nineteenth century certain bold and far-seeing students of medical science proposed a novel principle —novel at least in the scale on which it was then being proposed. It came to be known as "Homeopathic

Medicine" and was based on the principle that the best way to cure any disorder was to administer small controlled doses of medicines designed to produce the ills caused by the disease itself and thereby produce immunization to the full, virulent form.

This simple explanation is required for a principle which should long since have become a household word among social scientists had not our Establishment-controlled universities been too timid to allow researches in this area to be carried on freely—doubtless for fear of their interference with Defense Research projects. Therefore, Homeopathic Social Science is still in its infancy, and its truths remain almost inaccessible to students whose heads have been filled with traditional theoretical nonsense.

In essence, Homeopathic Social Science is simply a generalized and far more sophisticated version of the folk-tested "Doctrine of Signatures." That was the notion sometimes vulgarly summarized in the slogan "The Hair of the Dog That Bit You." In the 1860's this doctrine had a brief day of glory (or rather near-glory), thanks to the enlightened aid of the legislature and the people of the State of Michigan, who ordered the stuffy Regents of their university to establish a proper School of Homeopathy.* In this case—as in so

---

* Professor X's chronology appears to be slightly in error here. But the story, according to the best current authorities, is not substantially different from that which he recites. In 1867 the Michigan legislature, responding to the usual request for appropriations from the Board of Regents of the Univer-

many others before and since—the folk wisdom of *all* races was valiantly struggling against the "conventional wisdom" of the "learned" few. Homeopathic Medicine, once it had left the forum of the people themselves and had been plunged into the arena of the professional élite, was simply laughed away. Of course this is no different from the reception of the doctrine of inoculation and other great scientific truths on their first appearance.

In these 1960's, just one century later, the great doctrine of homeopathy is by way of being rediscovered. It should surprise no one that, instead of being announced and explored in the meetings of "learned" professional societies, it should have to be reannounced in an underground memorandum prepared by a brave

---

sity of Michigan, actually granted the university one-twentieth of a mill on every dollar of state property tax, but only on condition that a professor of homeopathy be added to the Medical Department. The Regents responded by offering to set up a separate School of Homeopathy anywhere (*except* in Ann Arbor) that a local community would offer buildings and endowment. But the university did not receive the tax money that year because the Supreme Court of Michigan held that the Regents had not complied with the clear condition on which the appropriation had been granted. Finally, however, as proponents of Homeopathic Medicine became more unpopular in the state, the State Supreme Court reversed this decision, and the University of Michigan received its tax funds. The Regents did actually establish a separate Homeopathic College in 1873, which had a controversial career until its incorporation into the University's Medical School in 1922. See Howard H. Peckham, *The Making of the University of Michigan* (Ann Arbor, 1967), pp. 59–60, 71–72, 77, 93–94, 147. ED.

few. But now we do unashamedly and most hopefully propose its bold and widespread application to the problems of New Democracy.

The first area in which Social Homeopathy shows its promise is that of "race relations"—or what we prefer to call ethnic fulfillment. Until the 1960's, the movements to ethnic fulfillment in the United States have been only crudely expressed. Our backwardness in this area is indicated by the fact that by so many Americans these movements were held in ill repute and were even considered to be a kind of social disorder. "White" (of course, as students of ethnic social science, we would no longer use so crude a term) "racists" were responsible for violence—lynchings, whippings, and other personal indignities—inflicted on persons they considered "non-white," and vice versa. Shortsighted, conventionally minded persons imagined that the way to prevent these disorders was to quench the racial enthusiasms that had caused them. Congress, responding to pressures from these unenlightened pressure groups, passed numerous laws. Among them were the so-called Civil Rights Laws, which we must now class with the Prohibition Experiment of the 1920's as a travesty on the very concept of legislation. And we can all remember the time, not so long ago, when our cliché-mongering Establishment "statesmen" were preaching such opiate doctrines as "assimilation" and "integration."

But nowadays one does not need to be a social scientist to see that the vigor of our society, the promise of New Democracy, lies in quite another direction. The pioneer work of the Ku Klux Klan, the Black Power Movement, the Black Muslims, the Black Students Union, the Black Panthers and their other courageous allies (to whom we have already referred) has revealed the New American Way. We now know that "racism" was an evil only when it was *not* universal. By inoculating each section of the society with the special brand of racism appropriate to it, we can hope to give a virile new vigor to all American life. Enthusiasm will match enthusiasm. Social Homeopathy will then have come into its own.

Wider applications of this profound, if superficially paradoxical, insight are not utopian. In fact it is a duty of all concerned social scientists to prove that they are not.

We already have some clues in the area of urban improvement. How many times have we been told by do-gooders, Establishment-oriented wolves in sheep's clothing (including settlement-house workers), and others that the cancer of our city is "the slum"? But who, other than a Social Homeopath, would have had the boldness to imagine that the "cure" of the big slum might be the little slum? So it is that the promising "Model Slum" project (promoted with local and state funds aided by matching Federal grants, and one of the few really productive government-supported enterprises) has shown its great possibilities, and may yet help us lead ourselves out of the urban wilderness.

Or—in quite another direction—what about the automobile? How often do we not read of the increase in traffic deaths due to the increasing number of automobiles? Is it not conceivable that if we could multiply our automobiles sufficiently rapidly and distribute them in large enough numbers, they would then become their own antidote? The actual problem may be not too many but too *few* automobiles on our highways. (Of course, this is only one additional item in the indictment of the automobile monopolists in their plots to keep their products out of the hands of the needy poor.) With enough more vehicles on the same highways at the same time might it not become impossible for any of them to move at a rate which would endanger life or limb?*

Social Homeopathy will help us, too, to untangle one of the most complex and confusing problems of our present corrupt society—the "problem" of "violence." Our most respectable social-science colleagues like a flock of conformist geese have gabbled that the problem of our society is "too much" violence. Which one of them has dared publicly to suggest that the real problem may be not "too much" violence but too little? May it not be, in accordance with the principles of Social Homeopathy, that the true remedy for a society ridden by more and more violence may actually

---

* This suggestion may not be entirely original with Professor X and his colleagues. See Victor Gruen's imaginative description of the planet "Autopia" in his *The Heart of Our Cities* (New York, 1964). ED.

be additional doses of violence (administered sporadically and universally) throughout the society?

The refusal to face this obvious possibility—indeed the reactionary refusal of social scientists to give a respectful hearing to the principles of Social Homeopathy—itself helps explain the confusion of vocabulary that plagues this much confused subject. The peculiar and widespread appeal of the concept of "Non-Violence" (and the need by students, blacks, and pacifists to use this as a euphemistic label for wholesome movements of violence) is explained simply by the fact that our Establishment social scientists have not yet progressed to the acceptance of a truly Homeopathic Social Science. When that essential step is taken —and it is our intention to help them take it—they will realize that what they have puzzled over under the label of "Non-Violence" is really and essentially nothing but Anti-Violence. And it will become increasingly apparent, as the doctrine of social antitoxin becomes more widely appreciated, that in the last analysis *all* Violence is actually Anti-Violence.

These are only a few of the interesting vistas opened up by Social Homeopathy. Who dares deny that in this direction, too, may lie solutions to our problems of crime, juvenile delinquency, pollution, and other forms of social disorder? *

---

* For some further suggestions on these points, see below, Appendix IV, "The Epiphenomenal Nature of Crime: Toward a Homeopathic Jurisprudence," and Appendix V, "A Note on the Origins of Civil Disobedience."

· IV ·
Toward a More Universal Society: Ways to Dissolve the Status Orientation of Our Institutions

———◆———

BUT, our readers will ask, what does all this bode for the university? When we began our Think-In we were naturally anxious to avoid undue concern for an institution so culturally loaded as a university. In the course of our discussions of the larger questions explored above, we formulated another axiom of New Democracy. What makes this axiom important is, of course, *not* that it describes the new and proper role of the university. For, although all of our authors happen in our corrupt society to be captives of the university, we hope that none of us has been so deeply corrupted as to fail to recognize that what happens to the university as such is, of course, of absolutely no consequence.

What *is* important is what happens to our whole society, and it has been *our* aim to encompass the whole society in our concern. In fact, it is this today rather extraordinary point of view that has led us to what may be one of the more fundamental propositions of New Democracy.

As we began to think about the place of the university in our society it gradually became clear to us that here, too, the basic problem is really nothing more nor less than the problem of status. The status orientation of our whole society—the two-cars-in-every-garage and the my-lawnmower-is-better-than-yours mentality—has not failed to corrupt our whole system of teaching and learning. This, of course, is not surprising. The surprising thing is that the discovery of this elementary fact (and its larger consequences) should have awaited the spotlight of our cadre.

Consider, for example, the very vocabulary in which we hear people every day talk about our educational system. They talk about the *"lower* schools," they talk about *"high* schools," and they talk about *"higher* education." Few if any of us have really faced the meaning of our words. What we are unwittingly describing (as social scientists should quickly recognize) is nothing more nor less than a system of *status*. We have been blind to this now obvious fact only because we are so accustomed to thinking of status as having to do only with individual people, or social classes, and not with institutions. But what we have had before our very eyes is an *institutional* status system.

When a student or a teacher in a "lower school" (or elementary school) refers quite casually to the teachers or students in a "high school," or when students or teachers in "high schools" talk about the students or teachers in institutions of "higher education," what are they *really* saying? They are really belittling themselves and in a sense groveling before the next higher institution on the institutional status ladder. Is this really anything more or less than *Institutional* Uncle Tomism? And is it, in the long run, really any better for a whole institution (with all its students and faculty) to grovel *en masse* than it would be for any one of its member-students or member-teachers to grovel individually? The answer to this should be obvious. If anything, *institutional* status orientation is even worse than individual status orientation because it is actually a kind of *wholesale* violation of the integrity and identity of individuals.

Our group has become convinced that what we are observing here is simply one example of a phenomenon as widespread as our whole society. The more familiar kind of status orientation (to which our society is beginning to wake up) is *vertical* status orientation (with students at the bottom, professors at the top, and other occupational groups in between). We have found it easier to recognize this phenomenon partly because it *is* vertical. The latest researches in small-group perceptional psychology confirm that we always find vertical phenomena most potent (e.g., in architecture, sex, etc.). This other, latent kind of status orientation that our cadre has now newly defined is no less a status orientation, but it is harder to recognize merely because it is *horizontal*. It appears horizontal in several senses and for several reasons: first, because the elements (in this case, institutions) that are part of this status system are discrete and are widely distributed through space; second, because of the widespread illusion (fostered by the media and especially by those persons on the higher rungs of this status ladder) that the hierarchy is indeed not a status hierarchy, but is somehow a value hierarchy which expresses an actual qualitative difference among the activities performed by the respective institutions.

What does all this add up to actionwise? We can draw the conclusions for New Democracy only if we generalize our description of this phenomenon. Yet this has been especially hard to pin down because it is so widespread and is embodied in individual prestigious institutions that until now no one has dared question.

The remedy to this hidden cancer of our society can be found only, we have concluded, in what some of us have called the "Principle of Social Non-Differentiation." The Establishment Principle is basically one of social differentiation. It arranges *all* the people in our society in a hierarchy of status, according to supposed intrinsic differences among them. Similarly, as we now have discovered, *all* institutions in an essen-

tially rotten society tend also to be arranged in a hierarchy of status. For purposes of clarity we have, to be
sure, called the one "vertical" status differentiation
and the other "horizontal" status differentiation. Basically they both express the same social phenomenon,
namely differentiation.

The problem of how to combat individual status
differentiation has been often and widely discussed,
and is hardly in need of our belaboring at this late
date. We do, however, think we have an action program against institutional status differentiation. And
if we are sufficiently persuasive, we will have won another skirmish in the never-ending battle against
Uncle Tomism on all fronts.

The only way to combat status differentiation and
status groveling among institutions is, obviously, to
destroy the differentiation. That is why we have hit
upon the guiding principle of Social Non-Differentiation. All institutions must be made more alike, not
only in *one* respect, but, hopefully, in *all* respects. In
New Democracy our object should be to use the
resources of social science to prevent people from
thinking better of some things (and hence of some institutions) than of others. (And, parenthetically, to
prevent any more thinking from going on in one institution than in another.) Translated into the vernacular,
this provides us the axiom "Everything is Everything;
Everybody is Everything." In a moment it will be
clear that this principle is neither so tautologous, nor

so paradoxical, nor so simple as it first seems. To begin with, I will explain its application to the university and the educational world in general, and then I will add a word on the concrete action-import of the principle for the whole society.

A great advantage of the principle is that it helps us, at the outset, to dispose of certain false assumptions. One false assumption is that, simply because our universities have failed in their traditionally assigned job of "teaching and study in the higher branches of learning," they therefore can*not* do everything else. Once we have firmly rejected the status orientation of institutions (in fact once we have rejected *all* types of horizontal status orientation), we have removed this bugbear. The principle of Social Non-Differentiation applied to the university provides us the guiding slogan "The World As University and the University As World."* When André Malraux wrote of "The Museum Without Walls" he was giving us a hint of this same principle in another field. When, indeed, will we have the wit to apply it to universities?

The simple consequence (displacing the so-called "liberal-arts" or "professional" or ROTC-dominated

---

* The Establishment may not be quite so hostile to this view as Professor X and his colleagues assume. See Harold Taylor, *The World As Teacher* (New York, 1969), which bears the indication on the reverse of its title page, "Research sponsored by the American Association of Colleges for Teacher Education under United States Office of Education Contract No. OE-6-10-116." ED.

universities well known to us in the past) would be the Universal University. Put a touch facetiously, such a New Democracy University would earnestly aim to be "All Things to All Men—Including Women and Children!" We have already seen some clues that this hope, too, is far from utopian. We have seen evidence within the last few years that our universities can indeed cease to be the bumbling "institutions of higher teaching and learning" they once were, and instead can take on a whole gamut of exciting new New Democracy roles. These roles include (among others too numerous to list): settlement house (in the Jane Addams tradition), employment agency, sexual experimentation laboratory, remedial-reading clinic, psychiatric ward, and, of course, training arena for revolutionary strategy and tactics. Building the Universal University will, then, quite obviously help dissolve the whole system of horizontal status orientation simply by making the university more like all other institutions in the society, and all other institutions more like the university.

This will help cleanse the society of its status obsession in two further ways. First, by making it easier to dissolve all the hierarchical distinctions among the universities. No longer will some students or teachers be able to lord it over others by saying that they come from the "Ivy League"!* No longer will there be the

---

* For a hint of some research possibilities in this area, see below, Appendix II, "A Note on the 'Ivy' League."

ridiculous cachet of "The Big Ten"! At long last we will break the oppressive stranglehold of so-called "accrediting" combines, like the North Central Association of Colleges and many others, which have been so important in preventing the free development of what under New Democracy would truly become People's Education for a People's Society. Then, and then only, in the finest non-status sense, *everybody* will receive the highest education.

As all universities (which then at long last will be People's Universities) become more and more alike, with no odious distinctions of quality among them, then, too, we can hope to see gradually the dissolving of distinctions between *all* the "types" of institutions in the Establishment's educational "system." This would mean, for example, that we would see more and more of our universities (no longer, we hope, to be called or, indeed, to *be* in any sense institutions of "higher" learning) giving more and more of their efforts to activities once condescendingly relegated to the "lower" schools (e.g., reading-readiness, "show-and-tell" sessions, fingerpainting, elementary arithmetic, African basket-weaving, ethnic cookery, etc., etc.). And *pari passu* we would hopefully see more and more of our young persons' schools (for ages five to thirteen, once condescendingly called "kindergartens," or "elementary" or "lower" schools) at long last devoted to activities once grovelingly relegated to "high" schools or "higher" education (e.g., demography, social anthropology, experimental biology, small-group psychology, critical study of mass-media, etc., etc.).

In this way, too, the struggle against horizontal status orientation would in the long run help dissolve many of the more disgusting forms of vertical (or individual) status orientation. Under these circumstances, for example, there would be no reason why a university "degree" (should it indeed be found desirable to retain this label for purely administrative purposes) could not be awarded at any or all stages of the program. This splendid idea deserves another few sentences. Nor is it as revolutionary as it seems. In fact it is in one respect at least a quite conservative idea, aimed to preserve the decorum of students and the peaceableness of student-faculty relations. For it would free students of the odium of "failing" "courses" and, hence, relieve them of having to resort to the indignity of intimidating the faculty with guns and knives in order to get their just rewards or the "degree," which is no more than their birthright.*

---

* On the indignity of preserving college degrees as rungs on the status ladder, Professor X (had he been a Shakespeare buff) might have recalled the following (from *Julius Caesar*, act II, scene 1, lines 22 ff.):

> *That lowliness is young ambition's ladder,*
> *Whereto the climber-upward turns his face;*
> *But when he once attains the upmost round,*
> *He then unto the ladder turns his back,*
> *Looks in the clouds, scorning the base degrees*
> *By which he did ascend.*

ED.

In all these ways, and probably in others as well, we would move several steps closer to the ideals of New Democracy. A total social fluidity (i.e., the eventual application of the Principle of Social Non-Differentiation to *all* our other corporate institutions, including the "family," the factory, and the whole oppressive apparatus of production and distribution, etc.) would soon accomplish for them what individual social mobility can accomplish for the individual. Namely, more rapid and more effective identity definition on the part of all members of the society and the abolishing of Uncle Tomism in each and every one of its forms.

· V ·
Toward the New Equality*

———◆———

THESE promising new conceptual tools open even wider vistas—toward the redefinition of the very ideal of equality on which all our institutions have supposedly been formed. We have asked ourselves—as we now ask our fellow social scientists and all concerned Americans—whether the time has not come for a revision of this fundamental ideal.

Formerly we aimed to make each American the equal of *other* Americans. But this point of view was itself status oriented and expressed a latent preoccupation with "better" and "worse" among people. That way of looking at equality may have been a necessary preliminary stage, though indeed a most primitive one,

---

* The unaccountable brevity (we might almost say abruptness) of this final section can only be explained by the desire of Professor X and his colleagues to indicate plainly that their enumeration was by no means exhaustive. Had they obtained from the Institute their requested grant for a Feasibility Study, they would then, doubtless, have been able to explore in greater depth what they see as the promise of New Equality. ED.

in our advance toward New Democracy. Perhaps the next stage of American idealism is better declared in the slogan "Each American Equal Not to Any Others, but Only to Himself."

Having arrived at this pinnacle of idealism, is it not now the duty of all social scientists—indeed of all men of wisdom and science together with all other Americans—to find ways of refining this, our central American ideal? Then may we not hope to find ways to apply the new equality to every nook and cranny of American life?

APPENDICES

On the Relation Between the E.Q. and the M.Q.

As the parameters of the E.Q. and the M.Q. are almost precisely the same, we have naturally toyed with the idea of devising a single "Omnium Quotient" comprising them both, which would even further simplify the task of administrators of New Democracy. It is worth a word here to explain why we passed up this temptation.

The answer is contained in the answer to still another question that must have occurred to a discerning reader. Are not both the E.Q. and the M.Q. *past*-oriented? Since "The Heritage of the Past" is so commonly used as a euphemism for "The Establishment," would this not mean, then, that *both* our new conceptual tools are in fact *Establishment*-oriented? Yet, on second thought, it becomes plain that this is not the case at all. It seems so only because our view of history, under the present regime of repressive tolerance, has misled us into identifying the *whole* past with the Establishment. True enough, both E.Q. and M.Q. *are* past-oriented. But they are emphatically *not* oriented to the Establishment past—rather to the truly relevant past, the ethnic, merit-qualifying essential past.

Since both E.Q. and M.Q. are social quantifications, it

is important also to note here a subtle difference in the two types of sociometrics that they represent. For this, better than anything else, will explain why we have here eschewed Occam's Razor,* and have preferred *two* quantifications to one. The E.Q. is, of course, a *descriptive* quantification, while, the M.Q., on the other hand, is essentially a *normative* quantification. To mix them would make nonsense, just as it would to add apples and oranges.†　Some segment of the M.Q., however, *is* undeniably descriptive (e.g., because it recites historical fact before drawing the normative conclusions).

The relationship between E.Q. and M.Q. is represented

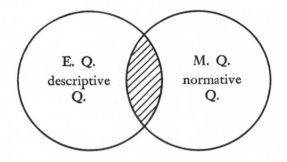

---

* The maxim that assumptions introduced to explain a thing must not be multiplied beyond necessity. Named after the English scholastic philosopher William of Occam (or Ockham) (1300?–1349). ED.

† Perhaps this is an example of a doctrinaire rigidity in our Professor X. A more flexible mind might have entertained the possibility that the mixing of apples and oranges, far from making "nonsense," actually produced a delicious new entity, i.e., fruit salad! ED.

in the topographical illustration on page 68, in which the shaded portion indicates the area of overlap.

It can instantly be seen that the area of overlap (of which the illustration can give, of course, only the roughest approximation) is hardly sufficient to justify merging the two whole calculations into a single quotient.

Nevertheless, the overlap is not to be ignored. When further researches are carried out and further applications explored, it is more than likely that interesting contributions will be made in characterizing (perhaps, too, in some new way, also quantifying) the varying nature of this "E.Q.-M.Q. Overlap Area" in different individuals and groups. It would be most surprising if some results were not found, at least roughly analogous to other kinds of overlap (for example, the so-called "Eaves Effect"— sometimes called by its full name, the "Eavesdrop Effect" —in public opinion statistics in general; or the overlapping of homosexual and heterosexual individuals in the whole society).

APPENDIX II

A Note on the "Ivy" League

———◆———

Students of the American language have long puzzled over the origin of the expression "Ivy League" to refer to certain institutions of "higher" learning. The common desk dictionary defines Ivy League as "a group of colleges (Brown, Columbia, Cornell, Dartmouth, Harvard, Princeton, Yale, and the University of Pennsylvania) in the northeastern United States forming a league for intercollegiate sports." And the widespread assumption has been that the cognomen "Ivy" was originally adopted because of the fact that these rich upper-class institutions consisted of substantial ancient buildings, generously covered with ivy (otherwise known as Virginia creeper, or, properly speaking, *Parthenocissus quinquefolia*). Less prejudiced investigation by a member of our group suggests another, somewhat less innocent, origin.

Our philological colleague observes that all the "Ivy" League institutions (with the exception of the University of Pennsylvania) are located in that part of the country (i.e., New England, New York, and New Jersey) that was most notoriously involved in the African slave trade.*

---

* Professor X's enthusiasm appears to have led him into an overstatement, which however does not entirely undermine his ingenious hypothesis. New England was *the* center of the slave trade in the colonial period, while New York and New

Many a colonial undergraduate playboy was educated, therefore, on the sweat and blood of the luckless blacks from whom his parents and grandparents had made vast fortunes.

The typical pattern of the slave trade was, of course, for the European or American to obtain his human loot by exchanging some valuable article with the helpless African chiefs or with the wily Arab flesh traders. And what was the most common commodity exchanged? *Ivory*, of course! Hence the colleges that were founded and supported by the so-called philanthropy of the slave traders quite naturally came, in course of time, to be called the "Ivory League." Then gradually, our linguist-sociologist explains, by the process (familiar enough to students of language) of what is technically called "back-formation" (e.g., that process by which "Welsh rarebit" became in spoken, and then in written, language "Welsh rabbit"), "Ivory" League became "Ivy" League.

An alternative explanation, which does not in the least challenge the novel implications of our linguist's discovery, is that the name "Ivory" League was adopted because the blacks themselves, who were, of course, the source of most of New England wealth, were commonly known in those days as "Black Ivory."

Jersey played only a minor role. But it is true that American colonial capitalism was becoming more cosmopolitan, and therefore it is quite conceivable that in these latter colonies, too, some substantial fortunes were made from that kind of commerce. See David Brion Davis, *The Problem of Slavery in Western Culture* (Cornell, 1966). The standard source is Elizabeth Donnan, ed., *Documents Illustrative of the History of the Slave Trade to America* (2 vols., Washington, D.C., 1930–35). ED.

There remains only one apparent flaw in this fascinating syndrome. What about the University of Pennsylvania? To be sure, Pennsylvania, being more inland than the other colonies mentioned above, tended to find the slave trade less accessible, and for that reason its capitalists found it harder to build quite so much of their superstructure on the flesh and blood of blacks. How, then, does the University of Pennsylvania fit into the picture? Or does this one deviant example actually vitiate the whole argument?

There are two possible explanations, either or both of which would cover this apparent exception. The economic history of the colonial period, as we all know, has been most imperfectly recorded. And the first possibility is that, in actual fact, Pennsylvania capitalists *did* have their hands deeply immersed in the blood of the slave trade—and to a much greater extent than the censored and doctored historical record might now suggest. We must not forget that that proto-Madison-Avenue-type Benjamin Franklin had actually helped found the university! Perhaps the Pennsylvania capitalists were unwittingly confessing their crimes through their spoken language.

But we must remember, too, that Pennsylvania had numerous Quakers in those days and that some of them were even allowed to attend the university. Is it not likely that it was these Quaker few who might have begun calling their institution one of the "Ivory League"? Perhaps it was in derision of the filthy source of the wealth behind their university. Perhaps it was their hope (which Quakers have exhibited throughout history) to *shame* their eighteenth-century fellow students into a recognition of the true rottenness of their society. If that was the case, then is it not plausible that a name that simultaneously happened to coincide with the guilt feelings of the dominant group and with the protest feelings of a courageous few became popular? Hence, in due course, the University of Pennsylvania called itself part of the "Ivy League."

We must not fail to note that the above is an example of how wisdom and conscience reside in the folk culture. Of this, as the example shows, the vital *spoken* language (by contrast with all forms of printed language) is the best witness. Hence, too, it is often the case that the least "learned" (in the printed-matter sense) classes are the richest repositories of true learning.

It may be worth adding a word on another example, even less trivial than the above. Why, for example, is "The White House" called *White* House? History books commonly say it is because the house was painted white after its destruction by fire in the War of 1812. But for this assertion there is not the slightest shred of evidence. Another explanation is much less flattering to that citadel of the Establishment.

There is a good deal of evidence to suggest that it was, in fact, originally known as "The White Man's House." (See F. J. Tompkins, *Africanisms and Americanisms in the Colloquial Speech of Western North Carolina*, New York, 1954, II, 67.) Then, by a familiar linguistic process of ellision-contraction (as "storehouse" became simply "store," as "Big Manor House" became "Big House," etc.), it was conveniently shortened into "The White House." So, unwittingly, then, whenever we refer to the

residence of the Chief Executive we are being more hon-
est than we might know. We are labeling him with the
stigma of racism, for which all our presidents (possibly
excepting President John F. Kennedy and his brother
Robert) have been the principal symbols and spokesmen.

Is "Retributive Merit" a Useful Concept?

We should, perhaps, make one qualification to our generalization that a person's M.Q. *never* changes and cannot be altered by anything he himself does in his own lifetime. Whether or not such a qualification is justified depends on what we think of the new behavioral factor which we might call "Retributive Merit." It has become increasingly prominent in the last two years. Retributive Merit might be defined as the merit that a person appears to acquire by an act aimed to express himself, to neutralize or make amends for past experiences of suffering. Examples would be the vandalizing of an exploitative elementary school, the shooting of repressive firemen in the ghettos, the burning of university library card catalogues, etc. Though it may be hard to draw the precise boundaries for such individual acts, it is clear enough by what criteria they should be defined.

At the outset, though, certain quantifying problems arise. We must not forget that while the Historical Equation assigns a *positive* value to past sufferings and indignities, it assigns a *negative* value to past pleasures and satisfactions. For any normal person, acts of retribution (especially if they are violent) are bound to give satisfaction and perhaps even pleasure (hence apparently requiring their negative value in the Historical Equation). How, then, can they possibly *add* to a person's M.Q., which is increased only by past sufferings? This is the dilemma.*

On the other hand it would plainly be unjust to calculate the Historical Equation in such a way that desirable acts of retribution—simply because they happen also to be pleasure-giving—actually might *subtract* from a person's accumulated past merit. This problem calls for a good deal of further investigation.

At this stage of our thinking, however, it would seem that the injection of the concept of Retributive Merit would only introduce needless confusion into our otherwise adequate Historical Equation. An ingenious colleague has suggested that an oscillating retributive factor be held in reserve as a kind of qualitative margin of error.

Oddly enough, it is this very margin of error that might turn out to be clinching evidence for the essential rightness of our *basic* concept of the Historical Equation. Our colleague reminds us that Claude Bernard, the famous French physiologist and neoethnicist, in his classic *Introduction to the Study of Experimental Medicine* (New York, 1927), pp. 115 ff., explains how a minor deviation in one of *his* equations led him to the discovery of glycogen.

---

* A dilemma that was vivid also to Shakespeare (see *The Merchant of Venice*, act IV, scene 1, line 215 ff.):

> *Wrest once the law to your authority:*
> *To do a great right, do a little wrong.*
>
> ED.

APPENDIX IV

The Epiphenomenal Nature of Crime: Toward a Homeopathic Jurisprudence

In the midst of the current hysteria about violence, "crime in the streets," etc., it may be in order for Homeopathic Social Science to bring some calmness to our thinking and some sharpness to our conceptualization.

A knowledge of the most elementary semantics would show us that a principal cause of confusion in our thinking is our tendency to reify "crime." We treat it as if it were an object out there, like a horse. This is very much the same error made in the hysterical 1920's (The Age of the Palmer Raids) and in the hysterical 1950's (The Age of the J. Edgar Hoover Raids) with respect to "communism." To all of us it should be apparent by now that the entity "communism" is indeed nothing but a figment in our minds—and it is here suggested that our thinking about "crime" today occurs in a precisely analogous epiphenomenal context.

Actually, our central confusion has arisen from our reluctance to face the uncomfortable fact that what we call crime is indeed not a primary fact at all, but purely and simply an epiphenomenon. By an epiphenomenon we mean, of course, "a phenomenon that occurs with and seems to result from another." This derivative and sec-

77

ondary character of crime may indeed be the key to the solution of our whole problem.

There have already been some hints of popular suspicion that crime does indeed have this character. Nowadays we commonly see and hear crime described as the result of poverty, of ghetto-living and slum conditions, of undernourishment, of poor education and underemployment, of alienation and frustration, etc. This is only another way of saying, all these surrounding circumstances are primary, while "crime" itself (i.e., the particular act of homicide, burglary, arson, rape, etc.) is only derivative or secondary. Folk wisdom seems once again to have hit upon an essential truth. Crime *is* indeed but a secondary and derivative fact. However, it does not really derive from primary facts of the type listed above, which our Establishment-minded jurisprudence has persuaded us to accept as causal.

What, then, *is* the primary fact from which "crime" is derivative? What is the one *sine qua non* without which crime could not exist at all? *The Law*, of course!

No law, no crime. Who ever heard of a society in which there were no laws, no law courts, no police brutality, no prisons, and yet in which there still was crime? It is the laws alone that describe crimes, that arraign the criminal, that "punish" the criminal, that take him to the electric chair or to the gas chamber, with all the attendant and brutalizing consequences.

In the early days of the American West, where a free and manly spirit ruled, where every man carried a gun to secure justice for himself and his loved ones, there was indeed precious little (if any) law. Even the idealized

Sheriff of Western-movie fame was usually so corrupt, so thoroughly in the pay of the big cattlemen or the big sheepmen, that he could hardly ever have been accurately called an agent of the law. Who was a "criminal" out there? Where was "crime"? Obviously there was none, and there could be none. For the good and sufficient reason that there was no law. Perhaps our Establishment-minded law-school-trained lawyers would say that out there *every* man was a criminal. But if that be so, then the New Social Science must retort: "Where every man is a criminal, no man is a criminal."

To return, though, from this historical footnote to our logical chain of argument. If all these plain facts are correct, it then follows that the primary causal factor is the law, and that crime is nothing but secondary, derivative, and epiphenomenal. The next step in our reasoning requires some intellectual courage (in the present repressive state of our society), but we must not hesitate. *The primary cause of crime, the one and only cause of crime, is law.*

From this radical conclusion there follow a number of revolutionary consequences, for the contemporary "problems of crime" and for the application of homeopathy to jurisprudence. If it is so obviously true that a society entirely without laws would be a society entirely without crimes, it is no less true that the *more* laws a society possesses, the *more* crimes it will be plagued by. But this is not the only—nor even the most important—logical consequence.

Our next step is so redolent with paradox that we find ourselves resisting its iron logic. But we must now recognize that the *more* crimes there are in a society the more *law-less* (i.e., law-free) the society tends to become. Do we not call a community "lawless" or "in danger of becoming lawless" (even when in one sense that community may be law-ridden, flooded by a plethora of laws) if in fact in that community the "crimes" are increasing apace. This is only another way of saying: Crimes tend to nullify laws. And whatever nullifies laws also, inevitably and in the very nature of the case, tends to nullify and decrease the possibility of more crimes.

How brilliantly relevant, now, do we find the principles of Homeopathic Social Science! The remedy for "crime waves," "crime in the streets," etc., at once appears. The remedy is not at all in *reducing* the quantity of crime, for that would in fact make the society less lawless (in other words, more law-full) and so would in turn only increase the probability—if not the certainty—of more and more crime. On the contrary, the answer is in the *increase* of crime, which *ipso facto* tends to destroy laws, to make the society less law-full, and in that very process tends in the long run to *decrease* crime, properly speaking.* From this basic insight we would hope that others better qualified might develop a full-scale Homeopathic Jurisprudence.

This whole approach is so novel that the opportunities it opens up for research have never even been envisioned, much less described. The only glimmer of understanding

---

* Professor X's labyrinthine logic is oddly reminiscent of the insight of a conservative English judge: "Civilization must be measured by the extent of obedience to the unenforceable." ED.

or insight comes, once again, from the folk wisdom. The recent widespread support of some enlightened neighborhoods (assisted here and there by hard-won government subsidies) for the "crime"-increasing youth gangs is then, indeed, a cheering augury. From the learned world, too, a few hints may be found in the following monographs: "Dutch" Spiegelbaum, *The Psychopathology of a Crook: An Intimate Portrait of My Friend Al Capone* (New York, 1942); Daniel Bell, "Crime As an American Way of Life" and "The Myth of the Mafia," in *The End of Ideology* (New York, 1960); Karl Gschicz, *Homes for the Homeless; Laws for the Lawless* (Amsterdam, 1946); Sigmund Freud, *Civilization and Its Discontents* (tr. Joan Rivière, London, 1949); Martin Buber, *Moses* (London, 1946).

APPENDIX V

A Note on the Origins of Civil Disobedience

Textbooks would have us believe that the toleration of some Civil Disobedience at different periods in American history has been an example of how freedom to dissent really is allowed in this purportedly liberal society. Consensus Historians and other Anti-Radical Historians are complacent over the fact that at times in our past a certain small number of Americans who happened to dissent from the prevailing imperialist warmongering were actually *not* shot. Examples most frequently given are Henry David Thoreau in the Mexican War, William Graham Sumner in the Spanish-American War, Rufus Jones and the Quakers in World Wars I and II, and, finally, the fact that only a minority of student dissenters have been killed or jailed for their opposition to the Vietnam War. A second look, and especially a more careful look at the history of Civil Disobedience in the United States, may help dispel our illusions.

When did the notion of Civil Disobedience first enter American capitalist mythology? The answer brings us to an interesting, and in some respects shocking, story. So far as we know, until now it has never been told.

Scholars of American Literature trace the origin of the

82

phrase "Civil Disobedience," and usually even of the idea, to an essay by Henry David Thoreau. That essay has been commonly known as "Civil [sic] Disobedience" (or more fully, "Essay on the Duty of Civil [sic] Disobedience"). Originally it was a lecture. Then it was first printed not as a separate booklet but as a chapter in Elizabeth Peabody's *Aesthetic Papers* (1849). In that volume it bore the title "Resistance to Civil [sic] Government." Until now this straightforward account has been universally accepted.

The actual facts apear to be quite otherwise. Although we cannot tell the long tale here in full, we can at least give a quick précis. This turns out to be one of the most fascinating literary detective stories of the century.

Our story begins in the White House, with the tribulations of the capitalist-puppet President James K. Polk (who had been born in North Carolina and then became a political boss in Tennessee). He had started the Mexican War in order to increase the power and profits of the Slavocracy. But that war was extremely unpopular in many parts of the country—so much so that even the opportunist Abraham Lincoln on one occasion actually pretended *not* to be in favor of it. As usual there were draft riots,* and there was widespread mutiny and disobedience in the armed forces. Notice, however, that the real peril was from *military* disobedience.

All these facts are only the essential general background. When we actually focus on the more specific

---

* Professor X appears here to be in error. There is no record that I have been able to find of the institution of a draft in the armed forces at that time. ED.

question of the origins of Civil Disobedience, what do we find? We find, to be sure, that as has been generally believed, Thoreau's essay *was* originally given as a lecture. When and where? It has always been known that the lecture was delivered to the Concord Lyceum sometime in late May or early June of that turbulent year 1846. Perhaps significantly, however, scholars of American Literature have not been overeager to explore the question of its precise original title, or the episode that followed its delivery. We are now ready to reveal these facts.

It happened that a young lady of Concord, Prudence Tompkins by name, was present in the audience. In that early day of the struggle for Women's Rights, Miss Tompkins (who plainly made up in courage what she may have lacked in education) was doing her bit by keeping a diary, fragments of which have lately turned up in the Women's Archives of Radcliffe College. For May 30, 1846, we find this entry:

> Today heerd a fine figger of a man—I think they calld him Thoreow—do his bit against this turrible war for the slavowners. He spoke up good and told the boys in awr army to stop obaying ther offissers. Whut he calld it was Military [*sic*] Disowbediens.

Next we find, in the unpublished correspondence of President Polk (in the Manuscript Room of the Library of Congress), a letter dated June 10, 1846. It is directed from the President himself to a Uriah Festerhaugh, his old friend and political supporter who lived in the vicinity of Concord. We quote:

My informants tell me that that vagrant would-be philosopher Thoreau aims to stir up trouble in the armed forces. I don't need to tell you that we have trouble enough already. You could do all of us (and your party) a service which will not be forgotten if you could somehow persuade the poor fellow to express his noble sentiments in some other language. For example, if you could persuade him, instead of pleading for Military Disobedience to plead for something else—say Citizens' or Civic or Civil Disobedience, then his rantings would be much less damaging.

With his usual political shrewdness, Polk added:

Not only that. If he made it plain he was appealing mainly to citizens at home (who make no difference anyway to the conduct of the war), we could show what freedom-loving democrats we were by not only tolerating him, but maybe even find some way to tame him into a minor bureaucrat. The post-office is already full of much worse trash.

The next thing we know, Thoreau's essay turns up in Elizabeth Peabody's *Aesthetic Papers* (1849) as a simple plea for resistance to "Civil Government." We can only surmise what must have happened in between.

There is more than a little evidence to suggest that the "wandering" habits of Thoreau, cryptically reported by Emerson and others, may have been due to the simple fact that Thoreau had been paid off for his surrender to Polk, having been rewarded by the job of postmaster of Concord.

All later reprints after the Peabody volume carry the title "On the Duty of Civil Disobedience." It is reported by scholars at Oxford that a recent Chinese translation at long last prints it under its proper title as a plea for "Military" Disobedience. But we have been unable to obtain a copy.

Here, then, is the origin of our much vaunted, nobly tolerated "Civil Disobedience." Instead of being an authentic example of a true toleration of dissent, it becomes a classic (if minor) case of repressive tolerance. Every time anyone boasts of joining a movement merely for "Civil" Disobedience, or of being in "the great tradition of Thoreau," he is in fact confessing Thoreau's original sin and unconsciously involving himself in that bribery which makes true freedom so hard to realize in our kind of society.

This leads us to another conjecture. How did it ever happen that the Civil War came to be called a "Civil" War? If there ever was a *Military* War, surely that was it. We will leave our readers to speculate on the rich possibilities (even in an area so overresearched as the Civil War) which this suggestion opens up.

POSTSCRIPT

A Sociology of the Absurd?
by
DANIEL J. BOORSTIN

———————◆———————

AS every civilization has its
own genius, so every age has its special talents and its peculiar vacuums. America today is not rich in either wit or
poetry. The characteristic intellectual achievements of
our time have been statistics and the social sciences. Our
great achievement in statistics (with electronic computers and data processing) is, of course, the Moon Land-
ing. The most vivid effect of our newly elaborated social
sciences—in the 1960's—has apparently been a national obsession with chaos. For one dramatic example of how we
have combined statistical techniques with social-science
knowledge we must look to that great American art—Ad-
vertising. There we do find bursts of wit and poetry.

But where else?

Another unlikely, but not altogether impossible, place
is the social sciences themselves. Where in our age have
men been better able to find new symbols, to announce
new rhythms, to encompass the world-complexity in a
mind-simplicity?

In literature some of the most characteristic works of our age, as everybody knows, have built a Theater of the Absurd. From Ionesco's *Bald Soprano* and *Rhinoceros* we learn things that our generation wants to know. What we seem unable to learn from the reasoned arguments of others we learn from their *reductio ad absurdum*.

Why not, then, a "Sociology of the Absurd?" This Professor X, whose application we have read, and the other solemn Professor X's in our world, may be able to tell us something that their more cautious colleagues cannot.

Index